"Autism doesn't come with an instruction guide. It comes with a family who will never give up."

— **Kerry Magro**

"Autism can't define me. I define autism."
— **Kerry Magro**

This book is dedicated to all the individuals with autism out there and their families who are trying to progress and grow each and every day. It's important to understand, like anyone else, we all have strengths and weaknesses. For those who keep fighting the good fight on our behalf, this is my way of saying thank you. Even if you don't see it, you are making a difference every day.
Keep it up.

www.mascotbooks.com

I Will Light It Up Blue!

For more information, please contact:
Mascot Books
620 Herndon Parkway, Suite 320
Herndon, VA 20170
info@mascotbooks.com

Library of Congress Control Number: 2018905439

CPSIA Code: PRT0220C

ISBN-13: 978-1-109555-491-3

Printed in the United States

Doug and Emma are twins, and their mom and dad love them more than anything else in the world. They are wonderful children, and their parents couldn't be more proud.

As Doug and Emma got older, their parents realized something wasn't quite right.

Emma wasn't speaking yet, and Doug was having issues with being touched by other people.

"What could this mean?" their mom asked their dad.

Doug and Emma's parents took the twins to visit different experts to find out what was going on. One day, their parents found out both Doug and Emma had something called "autism."

The doctor told them autism is a social and communication disorder that affects individuals differently. "If you've met one person with autism, you've met one person with autism," the doctor said. Even with this diagnosis, everyone still loved Doug and Emma for who they were.

As the years went on, Doug and Emma progressed because of the support from their parents. Along the way, they used different therapies to help. Emma started using an iPad to help her communicate, and Doug had a sensory brush to help him become comfortable with touching.

While some days weren't easy, their parents' unconditional love made them one of the happiest families in the world. Everything was going well.

Emma was on her iPad one afternoon when she saw something new. It was...
BLUE BUILDINGS!
PEOPLE WEARING BLUE!
SIMPLY PUT...
BLUE, BLUE, AND MORE BLUE!

Emma loved seeing blue everywhere. She scrolled to the top of the website, where she saw, "Light It Up Blue."

Wondering what that meant, she googled it and found out it is an initiative to celebrate people with autism. Emma went to her parents, typing in her text-to-speech app on her iPad.

"Mommy! Daddy! Look at everything blue!" she wrote. And that's when she typed something her parents weren't expecting...

Doug, Emma, and their parents sat down in the living room. "Autism is something countless people around the world have. It is a social and communication disorder, but it doesn't make that person any less of a person. You know how we know that's true? Because when you were very young, you both were diagnosed with autism," Dad said.

Their mom added, "We love you so much and always will. You may hear about a woman named Dr. Temple Grandin one day in your school. She reminds people that those with autism are 'different and not less.' You are no less than any other person. Always remember that."

Doug and Emma spent the night reading about **Light It Up Blue** and learning about another website called autismspeaks.org. They read about things like the early signs of autism, the definition of autism, and how autism has developed over time. They also read stories of people with autism just like them.

"I'm so glad to know we aren't alone," Doug said.
From that moment on, while learning more and more about autism
and what their diagnoses meant to them, they both became
autism advocates.

When **Light It Up Blue** showed up again on Emma's iPad, she and Doug decided they wanted to do something to make a difference. Doug asked his teachers if they would be willing to wear blue in their classrooms.

Emma asked her parents if they would buy blue light bulbs for their house.

Everyone jumped on board. **Light It Up Blue** prep was underway!

Emma and Doug sent cards to their friends and family to tell them the event had started.

Hi Everyone!

As many of you may know, we are on the autism spectrum. We hope you will go to websites like autismspeaks.org to learn more about autism and to spread awareness throughout our community.

We will also **LIGHT IT UP BLUE** by wearing blue and lighting our home up blue. We hope you will go blue to help start a conversation about autism!

We have autism, but autism can't define us. With your help, we can help the world become more educated about people with autism like us. Thank you!

Love,
Doug and Emma

Emma and Doug received praise as call after call came in. They were overwhelmed with happiness. The next morning, Doug and Emma rushed to their parents' bedroom and jumped on the bed, chanting, "Selfie time! Selfie time! Selfie time!"

As they got ready for school, their mom surprised the family with puzzle piece chocolate pancakes for breakfast! Puzzle pieces are the international symbol for autism awareness. "I cut them myself," Mom said.

Mom and Dad took Doug and Emma to school, where kids and teachers in blue clothing greeted them. Doug and Emma were so excited. Their school had decided to **Light It Up Blue!**

In the evening, Dad drove them around the neighborhood. All of the houses were lit up blue!

"You helped make all of this happen," Mom told Doug and Emma. "You will learn this as you get older, but when you are a part of a community, like the community who helped make our town go blue tonight, anything is possible as long as you have each other."

"What did you enjoy most about **Light It Up Blue?**" Dad asked.

"I enjoyed all the blue!" Doug exclaimed.

"Me too, me too!" Emma agreed. "And I liked seeing the support of people with autism like me. It made me realize I'm not alone."

"Couldn't have said it any better myself," Doug said. "I can't wait to Light It Up Blue again next year."

Epilogue

In 2007, the United Nations proclaimed April 2nd as World Autism Awareness Day, which coincides with the global awareness initiative **Light It Up Blue** that started via Autism Speaks. After reading this story, we hope you will consider lighting it up blue in your local communities! You can learn more at www.autismspeaks.org.

About the Book

I Will Light It Up Blue is the story of Doug and Emma, twins on the autism spectrum, who find out about an initiative called Light It Up Blue that happens on World Autism Awareness Day and throughout the month of April to help shine a light on people with autism. Throughout the story, Doug and Emma show the readers what it means to believe in something, how to inspire others, and how to help spread awareness of autism.

About the Author

Kerry Magro is an award-winning professional speaker and bestselling author who is on the autism spectrum. Nonverbal until two and a half years old, he now travels the country sharing his story and highlighting people impacted by a diagnosis by sharing their story with the world.

Kerry worked at Autism Speaks from 2013 to 2017 as their Producer of Social Media and Digital Content before fulfilling his dream of self-employment.

Kerry's first two books *Defining Autism from the Heart* and *Autism and Falling in Love* were on Amazon bestseller lists.

You can read more about how you can work with Kerry at kerrymagro.com or contact him at kerrymagro@gmail.com.

Follow Kerry's journey on Facebook at Facebook.com/Kerry.Magro.

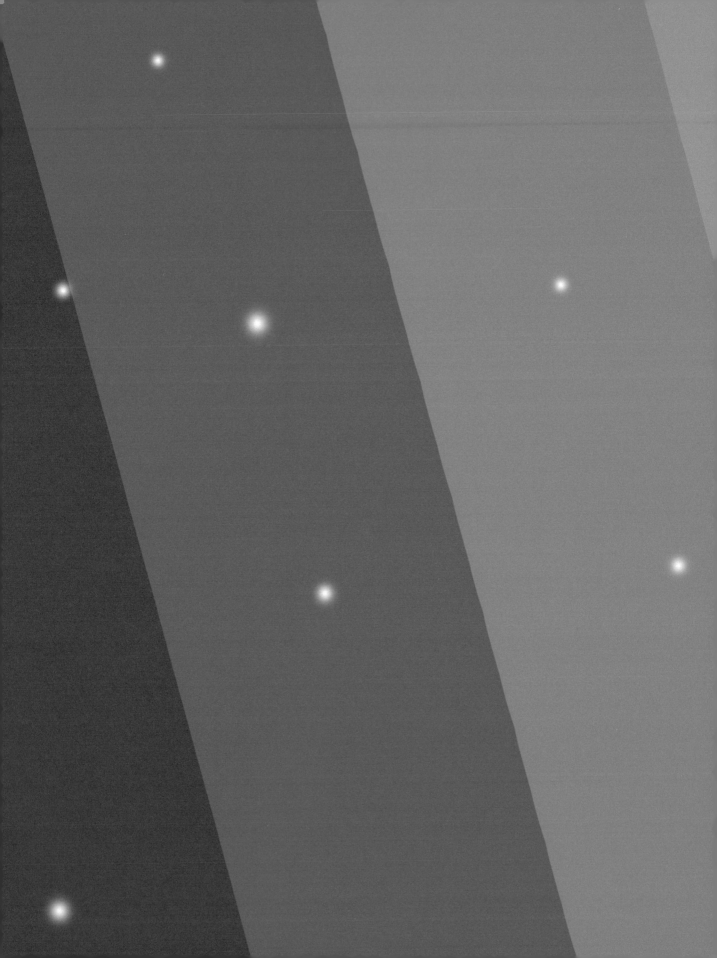

Made in the USA
Columbia, SC
23 October 2024

44612006R00022